The Four Basic Steps in

Window Tinting Your Car

The Four Basic Steps in

Window Tinting Your Car

by Armando Acosta

About the Author

Armando Limon Acosta Jr. has spent ten years professionally window tinting, the last eight of which were spent at a local Luxury car dealership in Las Vegas, where he started the Window Tint department and is in charge of in-house paint protection. Inspired by his own beginnings in the industry, author Armando Limon Acosta Jr. decided to write The Four Basic Steps in Window Tinting Your Car to help others who have been in a similar situation. Long before he became a professional, he was a normal high school student who wanted to tint his windows. However, it wasn't until after he got a job at a local tint shop that he began to unravel the mysteries of window tinting. With an urge to help beginners, Acosta created this guide to ensure everyone would have a hands-on resource they could go to. These tips and tricks might have taken him years to learn, but with this amazing guide, beginners can learn them in no time.

2012 Mike Green

Acknowledgments

First of all, I would like to thank everyone that has helped me in the process of this book, and I would also like to thank Brett Green for helping me start the book with the introduction, Thanks man. I would also like to thank my kids, Melissa, Milena, and Michael Acosta for being the best kids anyone can ask for; furthermore, I would like to thank Maria, my girlfriend, for giving me all the love and support; in conclusion, I would like to dedicate this book to Sandy and Shasta Acosta, gone but not forgotten.

Table of Contents

Chapter 1

An Introduction to Window Tinting

Benefits..................................12

Cosmetics..............................14

Environment.........................16

Chapter 2

An Introduction to the Tools and Film

Heat Gun...............................20

Blue Max................................22

Dryer Sheets.........................24

Chapter 3

Step One Cutting the Film

Solution Mixture...................30

Front Windows......................33

Rear Windows........................37

Back Window.........................43

Chapter 4

Step Two Shrinking the Film

Side Windows..........................48

Back Windows.........................51

Chapter 5

Step Three Prepping the Windows

Side Windows.........................56

Quarter Windows....................59

Back Windows........................62

Chapter 6

Step Four Installing the Film

Side Windows.........................66

Quarter Windows....................75

Back Windows........................76

Chapter 1

An Introduction to Window Tinting

My objective is to present a simple, easy-to-understand philosophy of window tinting that can aid you in replicating a professional job. Window tinting is comparative to cooking, with the right recipe, timing, ingredients, and tools, anybody can achieve success. Akin to cooking, there are as many chefs as there are tinters, many of whom are simply a product of their teachers and recipes they have learnt and studied from over time. I hope you can learn and add to my recipe, in time making it your own.

In addition, this book will cover the essential tools every novice and experienced tinter will need to complete a successful job and their specific applications. This will be followed by step-by-step instructions on applying tint to the sides and rear of your vehicle. Each step in the following chapters should be followed carefully and exactly to ensure optimal efficiency.

Benefits...............................12

Cosmetics............................14

Environment.........................16

Benefits

Window tinting is a skill that can be acquired by anyone. Proper window tinting simply requires interest, a fair amount of motivation, and a good source of information. The information I intend to provide you with is a reflection of my 10 years of professional experience, during which I have worked with many skilled tinters and documented a variety of their habits and tricks while subsequently developing my own method that is streamlined to be both efficient and effective.

The following is a short list of reasons why one would wish to take up the art of window tinting:

- Trade, a job providing a very good source of income
- Extra cash as a side job
- Prospect of opening your own tint shop
- Avoiding the expensive cost of having a tint shop tint your windows

There are many reasons why you would want to learn to window tint your own car. And there are many more reasons why you would want to get into the business, but here are a few benefits on why you would want to add tint to your car or anyone else's.

The first benefit that I promote is heat rejection. Heat rejection will benefit an automobile in a variety of ways. By keeping cool air in and hot air out, you reduce the need to use the vehicle's air-conditioner saving on fuel necessary to power it. In addition, cooler cars and engine parts tend to run more efficiently, thus cutting down on fuel, which will save you money in the long run.

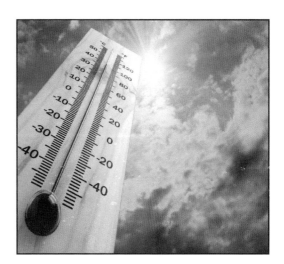

mycola heat @ 123rf stock photo

beawolf @ 123rf stock photo

The second benefit is cosmetics it enhances a vehicle's image. There are a variety of shades and colors of tint to choose from, and they can make an ordinary car look fast or important within a few hours. Tint will also provide you with valuable UV protection that will both protect your skin from the sun and your interior from fading. It will also preserve leather seats, preventing them from drying out or cracking prematurely.

Tinting your car can also add value to it. A little known secret of used car dealerships is that they tint many used vehicles in order to move them more efficiently. This has proven to be a very cheap and effective strategy that you can also apply to your own car, or cars, if you plan to sell them in the near future.

m600maxx @ 123rf stock photo

rioblanco @ 123rf stock photo

Tinting your vehicle can also add a great deal of privacy and security to your belongings. If thieves can easily see your DVD player in the headrest, or a new expensive car stereo in clear visibility, you are more likely to have your car broken into than the person who invested in tinting their car. This can also protect women and children from nighttime predators looking to hijack some easy, helpless victims by not allowing such deviants to know who is driving the car.

Yuri Arcurs @ 123rf stock photo

Environment

When tinting any vehicle, it is of the utmost importance that it is in a closed environment free of any dust or strong drafts of air that may carry dust. Just as a top chef would keep their kitchen clean and clear of any unwanted elements, you should address your tinting bay or garage with the same level of care. I would make sure that the wind is NONEXISTENT; any tinter will tell you that wind is enemy number one, both for its ability to carry dust and because it can easily blow away your fragile and expensive film.

 Next is the placement of glass along the walls of your environment in areas you deem most convenient to your working proximity. The purpose of this is to have an area to cut, measure, and prepare tint for immediate placement on the car window thereafter. This is a very important utility that almost any professional tinter uses on a daily basis; do not leave out this crucial step in your tint work. If you plan to purchase panes for a professional tint shop capable of tinting a wide variety of vehicles, it is recommended that you get at least two panes of glass that are at least 48" in length by 48" in width. You want the panes of glass in your shop to be large enough to place an entire piece of back window tint (usually the largest cut) onto the panes of glass, and this measurement should be big enough to fit most back windows.

Water is the last element that you should have on hand, in the form of a spray bottle or a nearby water faucet. Water is important to help keep tint pliable and to prevent unnecessary creases and wrinkles when handling tint with your hands, or in the actual process of the application.

nikkytok @ 123rf stock photo

Chapter 2

An Introduction to the Tools and Film

My objective in this chapter is to introduce you to the tools that I use to install the window tint. There are many more tools available in the market today, but I would highly advise you to use the tools I use until you feel comfortable before you start experimenting with other tools. I will be numbering each tool, so you can refer back to this chapter anytime you need to.

cla78 @ 123rf stock photo

Heat Gun.............................20

Blue Max............................22

Dryer Sheets.......................24

Tools

1

Heat Gun

I use the heat gun to shrink the side windows and back film, and I use it to burn out dirt trapped between the film and windows. I also use it to burn out creases.

2 I use the stool to roll around the car while I'm installing the film. It just makes things a lot more comfortable.

Roller Stool

Tinting Belt

3

I use the belt to store tools I use all the time, that way I stay more organized. I'm going to make a red frame around it, and I will make a red frame around all the tools I store in it all the time. This will help give you an example of the tools I use most frequently.

4 3.5" Yellow Turbo

I use the smaller turbo for quarter windows.

5 5" Yellow Turbo

I use the bigger turbo to install the side windows.

The Yellow Chizler

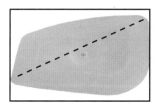

The Yellow Chizler

I use the Chizler for a lot of different things. I use the whole Chizler to burn things out that are trapped in between the film and glass, usually small amounts of dirt and little hairs. And here is a little secret I will share with you; I cut the Chizler in half, and with the half of the Chizler I use it to install the film under the gasket of the side windows. I also use the half of the Chizler to loosen up the gaskets of the quarter windows before installing them. With the white Teflon, I never use it whole. I usually always cut it in half, and I use the half of the white Teflon for installing film under the gasket of the side windows too; in addition, I always use it to seal the film around the edges of the side windows. The white Teflon is good because it's flexible and it slides on the film with out scratching it; just remember to sand both of the tools after cutting them with fine sand paper.

4" White Teflon Card

After you're done cutting the Chizler and Teflon, you will want to sand them smooth.

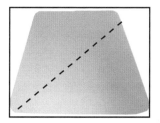

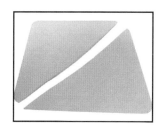

4" White Teflon Card

Tools

10 Single Edge Razor Blade (100)

The blades are meant to be used with the retractable razor blade to clean the side windows.

11 Retractable Razor Blade

The retractable razor blade is meant to hold the blades while cleaning the side windows—beats using your fingers.

12 NT PRO A-1P Red Dot Knife

The Olfa knife is meant to cut out window tint and clean gaskets.

13 Olfa Stainless Blades (50)

The Olfa blades are meant to be used with the Olfa knife. The stainless steel blades are meant not to scratch glass.

14 Pro Handle

The Pro Handle is meant to be used with the blue max.

15 Blue Max

The Blue Max is meant to be used with the Pro Handle. It squeegees more water out than the yellow turbo.

16 Push Stick

I use the push stick to burn out dirt and creases.

17 25oz. Spray bottle

The spray bottle is meant to hold window tint solution.

18   Slim Foot

I use the slim foot to push out water at the bottom of the back window.

19   4" Black Teflon Card

The black Teflon is used to shrink side and back windows.

20   Side Swiper

The side swiper is meant to get water out at the bottom of the back window.

21   Super Prep Towel

The rags are meant to clean gaskets. They are lint free.

22   Microfiber Cloths

I use the microfiber cloths to wipe the side of car down and the inside door panels and windows.

23   Basic White Scrub Pad

The scrub pad is meant to clean the back window without damaging the defrosters.

24   Window Switch Tape (1000 count)

The tape is meant to keep customers from rolling their windows down too early.

25   Door Upholstery Remover

If removing door panels, the upholstery remover is very helpful.

Tools

White China Marker

26 I use the white china marker to mark on the film and on the windows.

Baby Shampoo

27 The baby shampoo is meant to be used with water to make your main solution. Just add a drop of it in a 25 oz. bottle.

Dryer Sheets

28 The dryer sheet is meant to be used with the back windows to keep static electricity away, when shrinking.

Measuring tape

29 The measuring tape is meant to measure the windows.

8" Circle Template

30 I use the 8" circle as a ruler and to cut out perfect circles when needed.

Automotive Bull Dozer

31 The bull dozer is meant to get in between a back light that can't be removed for the back windows.

Light

32 I use the light to brighten the back window when I'm cutting it out.

600 grit Sand Paper

33 I use sand paper to sand the tool, so they dont scratch the film.

Now that I have introduced you to the tools that I use all of the time, I will tell you where you can buy them. I usually buy them from a distributor like Suntek, American Standard Window Films, DigiCut System, and Solar Guard; you can find them on the internet. Any of these distributors carry tools but they also carry film as well. I also like to use 44 tools.com. They carry a lot of different tools, and you can find them on the internet too.

An Introduction to the Film

There are a lot of different shades out there, but I will talk to you about the main three that I use. I use 05%, 20%, and 35%. The percent represents the amount of light being transmitted through the film, so the darker the film is the less amount of light that is transmitted. In the picture 1.1 the 05% shade is considered the limo, the 20% shade is considered the dark, and the 35% shade is what we call the middle shade. There are more shades out there and it really just depends what you are looking for. If you are not sure what you want to buy, I would just call the distributors and ask them for samples of the shades that they offer and they will send you a packet. Before deciding on the shades, I would recommend you to find out the laws in your state, so that it can help you figure out what you need.

1.1   5%   20%   35%

I would recommend going to tintlaws.com or tintdude.com they have a list of states and their laws concerning window tint, but I will give you a little sample of the laws. If you do not see your state on here, go to the web site to find out the law in your state before you tint yours or anyone's car. And as the web site states keep in mind that as things change, the data might not always reflect the latest changes in your community. There have been cases where tint laws and regulations differ slightly from region to region, in the same state even. This is mostly due to the way these laws and regulations are interpreted by each district. Because of this, we always advise and encourage you to turn to your local authorities last, in order to ensure that the information you have reflects the laws enforced in your specific area.

STATE	FRONT SIDES	REAR SIDES	BACK WINDOW	VISOR
AZ	33%	ANY%	ANY%	AS1
CA	70%	ANY%	ANY%	4"
CO	27%	27%	27%	4"
FL	28%	15%	15%	AS1
HI	35%	35%	35%	4"
IL	NO	ANY%	ANY%	6"
IN	30%	30%	30%	AS1
KS	35%	35%	35%	AS1
KY	35%	18%	18%	AS1
NE	35%	20%	20%	AS1

STATE	FRONT SIDES	REAR SIDES	BACK WINDOW	VISOR
NV	35%	ANY%	ANY%	AS1
NJ	NO	ANY%	ANY%	NO
NM	20%	20%	20%	AS1
NY	70%	70%	ANY%	6"
NC	35%	35%	35%	AS1
OH	50%	ANY%	ANY%	70%
OR	35%	35%	35%	6"
TX	25%	25%	ANY%	AS1
UT	43%	ANY%	ANY%	AS1
WA	35%	35%	35%	6"

One more thing that you might want to know about window tint is the heat rejection and the UV protection that each film offers. When you get your packet from each distributor, it is good to do your due diligence and learn more about each of these two subjects. The more you know about the film and the benefits they offer the better you will be able to sell it to the customers or be better equipped to pick out what film you need on your car.

Chapter 3

Step One Cutting the Film

In this chapter, I will teach you how to cut the film. This is one of the four basic steps in installing window tint to your car. I advise you not to skip a step because it can make it harder for you in the end.

Solution Mixture...................30

Front Windows.......................33

Rear Windows.......................37

Back Window.........................43

The first thing you must know is the mixture used in installing the film. In the mixture you want a 25 oz. bottle and just a drop of baby shampoo. You will always use this mixture.

Before you start cutting, I would recommend cleaning all of the windows, even the back window, with the mixture of baby shampoo. You will want to clean the windows by spraying your solution and then wiping the windows with your squeegee to remove dirt and anything stuck on the outside of the windows that can damage the film.

Another thing that you must know before we start the cutting process is the film; you can either use a 40" roll or a 20" roll. In my examples, we will be using the 40" roll because you can always get two 20" sides from the 40" roll.

40" roll

The next thing you will want to do is measure the length and width of the windows so you know how much you have to cut out.

This is the shiny side.

This is the dull side, also known as the liner.

You will also want to know what side to peel. Window tint film always has two sides to it, a dull side (the liner) and a shiny side. The dull side is the side that comes off and you will not be using. The shiny side is the side that will be installed.

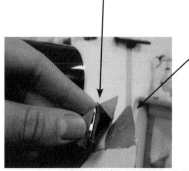

CONTINUED ON NEXT PAGE

In this picture, I am using the 40" roll, which has been cut out big enough to cover the whole window and a little more. You also want the shiny side of the film facing you.

40" side

Shiny

In this picture, I folded the film in half to make two 20" sides. Now you should have the dull side facing you.

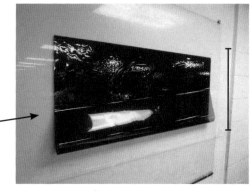

Two 20" Sides

Dull

Now with your Olfa knife cut the film in half.

After you have cut the film in the middle, you end up with two sides. When you are working with a sedan, most of them are smaller than 20" in height. If you're working on a truck, it could be bigger than 20", so that's when you would want to skip this part and use the whole 40" side.

This is a straight trimmed side.

How to cut out the front windows

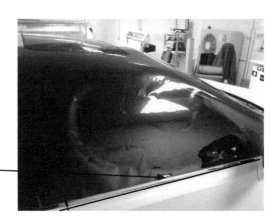

You will want to use the straight side of the film for the bottom cut. By doing that, it is one less cut you have to do.

Now, you will want to trace the front corner of the front passenger window with the china marker.

26

CONTINUED ON NEXT PAGE

After marking the front corner, you will want to mark the other side of the film with the china marker. You will have both sides marked, so now you will want to cut out the top part of the window.

You will have extra film on the side and the top of the window. You will want to cut it off so that it is easier to make the top cut. All the extra film is extra weight you don't need.

1. **2.** **3.**

Tack the film down with the black Teflon in the middle of the window. You will be rolling the window down, and you don't want the film sliding down or up. If the film slides down, you will end up with a big gap on the top of the inside of the film.

Lift the film up from the bottom of the window, so that it doesn't crease while you roll down the window with your other hand.

After you're done cutting out the extra film, tacking the film down, and rolling the window down, you are now ready to cut the top edge of the window.

The way I cut it is by putting the edge of the knife against the window and using the window as a guide all the way down until I have the perfect cut.

Edge of knife on window.

CONTINUED ON NEXT PAGE

This is what the cuts should look like
after the steps from above.

But we are not finished. You will want
to cut on the outside of the markings
to finish the sides.

Use finger to make
round edges.

And this is what the finished product
should look like. If you folded the 40"
roll and cut both of them out following
the steps above, you should end up with
two front windows.

How to cut out the rear windows

It's really much the same as cutting out the front windows, but I will go through the steps again with you. Here I am measuring the length and width of the window.

After you're done folding the 40" roll and cutting out the two sides, place on rear window.

This should be your straight side.

CONTINUED ON NEXT PAGE

Mark the two sides of the window, so you know where to trace.

Cut off any extra film from sides.

Tack down film, so that it doesn't slide when you roll down the window.

Hold film away from window
at the bottom, so when you
roll down the window, it won't
crease.

Roll the window down.

Place the edge of your Olfa knife on
window and cut using the window as
your guide.

CONTINUED ON NEXT PAGE

Use the window as a guide and cut all the way to the other end of the window.

Place the film on glass and cut on the outside of the marks you made with the china marker. This is where you can also use your ruler to make a better cut and your finger for round edges.

30

Cut out side of line.

Use the 8" Circle Template ruler to help with the straight lines.

You can use your finger to make a round edge.

This is what your finished side of the rear windows should look like. Sometimes you will have to adjust the cut and cut a little smaller or bigger depending on the installation. You really won't know until you install it, but as long as you followed my instructions and the film doesn't slide on you while cutting it out, it should fit just fine.

How to cut out the quarter windows

Have two sides ready, and then place film on top of quarter window.

CONTINUED ON NEXT PAGE

1.

Trace film around the quarter window with the china marker. After tracing the cut with your Olfa blade, you should have a perfectly cut quarter window.

2.

This is what your quarter window should look like when you are done.

3.

4.

How to cut out the back window

For the back window, I pick up the 40" roll and unroll it until it fits the whole back window. For me this is the fastest way to get the back window started.

This is the back window ready to be cut.

CONTINUED ON NEXT PAGE

The first thing that I do is cut out a hole around the antenna.

Shrink first, pg. 51.

- -

Before you continue, I would recommend shrinking the film first and then come back and continue.

This is what the back window should look like after it has been shrunk and is ready to be cut.

I would get the light and put it in the back to light up the matrix. When cutting out the back window, you will want to cut out an eighth bigger than the matrix.

This is the matrix. ——————

Get your Olfa blade and start cutting around the matrix; with the light in the back it should be no problem.

When you don't have a light to help you cut out the back window, you can always use your finger as a guide. Just put your Olfa blade next to your fingers and follow it down. Use more fingers if the matrix is ticker.

This is what your back window should look like when you are done cutting it out.

Chapter 4

Step Two Shrinking the Film

In this chapter, I will teach you to shrink the film. The whole reason for shrinking the film is to mold the film to the glass. By doing this you have less problems when you install the film

Side Windows..........................48

Back Windows.........................51

Shrinking

How to shrink the side windows

The first thing you should know is the way the film is designed to shrink. You can only shrink it one way. The film is designed to shrink vertically and not horizontally.

OK, if we look at this 40" piece of film, it can only be shrunk vertically.

We will start out by placing the pattern you cut out from step one an inch or two away from the side gasket and an inch or two away from the lower gasket.

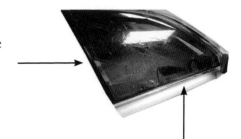

Tack down the side and the top of the
film trapping the fingers in the middle of
the window.

1.

⑲

Side

2.

3.

Top

    After tacking down the film, you should have all the extra film in the middle
of the window that you will want to shrink. The purpose of shrinking the film is to
get the film to be molded exactly to the window, so it fits like a glove when you install
it. By doing this now, you will have less problems when you install the film to the
window, and less fingers and things you don't want to mess around with once the film
is installed.

This is an example of a finger.

This is exactly what you want to shrink, so
get your heat gun out; it's time to shrink.

CONTINUED ON NEXT PAGE

Shrinking

When shrinking, you will want to blast your heat gun on high, and all you want to do is place it on top of the finger. Shortly after that, come down with your black Teflon and slide over it to make it flush with the window. By heating up the film, you're able to make it soft, and that's when you're able to manipulate it to form it like the window.

If you get comfortable shrinking, you can also shrink two sides at the same time, just make sure that the window is not too curvy.

This is what it should look like when it is done: flush with the window.

How to shrink the back window

This is where you will want to get your dryer sheet out. I spray a little of my solution on the glass, making sure it's already clean from dirt, and then I wipe the whole back window with the dryer sheet. It will leave a gloss all over the window. We use it to keep static electricity from sticking to the window and film while we shrink it. You might want to try it with and without the dryer sheet just so you can see the difference.

After applying the dryer sheet and allowing it to dry, you are ready to measure the film and cover the window with it. I usually just take the 40" roll and lay it across the whole window.

Cut around Antenna.

Make sure to cut a hole for the antenna and to cut an inch all the way around the glass. You don't want the film touching anything when you are shrinking it because it can mess up your shrink.

Make sure it doesn't touch the side.

CONTINUED ON NEXT PAGE

Shrinking

Now that you have cut out the antenna and the side, you want to tack down the film like an H. Tack down the film with your black Teflon vertically and then horizontally, just like in this picture.

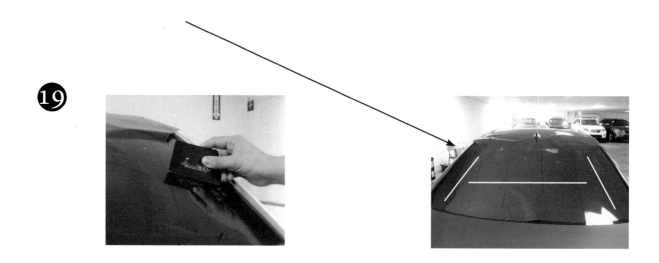

After the film is tacked down, you're ready to shrink the back window. You will need your heat gun and black Teflon.

In this diagram you will want to start shrinking on the 1.1 and follow it until 1.5, then you will follow the white arrows right and then left. The green arrow represents the way the film can be shrunk, and the white arrows represent the direction after the numbers you're supposed to follow. Each circle represents two inches by two inches. I am recommending that you shrink two inches by two inches at a time. Start shrinking 1.1 two inches at a time and then move to 1.2 and so on until you start following the white arrows all the way to the bottom of the window. You will also do the same for the top shrink starting on 2.1 to 2.5 and following the white arrows. The main advice I can give you relating to the back window is to shrink a little at a time and keep it all balanced.

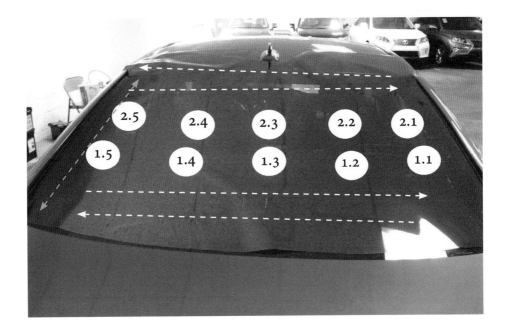

Use the top of the film to help you shrink the top part. By holding the top film, you can keep the shrink going all the way to the end of the film, which should be more than enough.

Chapter 5

Step Three Prepping the Windows

In this chapter I will teach you how to prep your windows properly before installing the window tint. This chapter is critical in making your install look professional. The cleaner your install looks, the more jobs you will get. In the end, this is what you will be judged on: the clean look.

Side Windows..........................56

Quarter Windows....................59

Back Windows........................62

How to clean the side windows

The first thing you want to do is spray the window with your mixture.

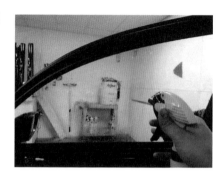

The second thing you want to do is extend your Olfa blade out as far as it can go and slide it in between your gaskets, the side gasket and the bottom gasket. There is usually a lot of dirt trapped in there that you will want to scrape off. You will have less dirt in new cars, but I still recommend doing it with new cars. In older cars you will want to clean it a few times, maybe two times, before applying your film. It just depends on how dirty the car is, but older cars are known of being dirtier.

After you have cleaned your gaskets with your Olfa blade, you will want to get out your retractable razor blade and start cleaning the right side corner of the window, cleaning it all the way to the other side of the window. You will want to clean the entire window without missing a piece of it. The purpose of doing this is to remove anything that is stuck to the window, like dirt, food, or whatever might be on it. And in this step, I will share another tip with you. Sometimes things are invisible to the eye, so that's when I will use my hand. You can rub your hand on the glass and sometimes feel things you normally wouldn't be able to see.

Roll the window down and start from the top right corner all the way to the other side of the window.

Spray the window down with your solution again.

CONTINUED ON NEXT PAGE

Cleaning

Get your rags out and tear off a sheet. With the sheet, rub the top side, the side and the top part of the window. By doing this you are removing any dust or dirt that is waiting to ruin your installation.

1.

21

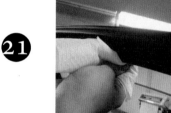

2.

3.

Spray your window down again and squeegee it, top first and then down.

1.

17

2.

5

3.

After cleaning your window, you will want to spray the sides down. By doing this you are flushing any leftover dust or dirt down the gasket. Once you're done flushing it, you are ready to install the film.

How to clean the quarter windows

For the quarter window, it's the same concept as above; you will want to spray it with your solution.

CONTINUED ON NEXT PAGE

I usually start out by cutting an eight of the gasket off so that I can slide the window tint into it without allowing light to come through.

After you spray the window with your solution, and cut an eight of the gasket off, you will want to loosen up the gaskets if they are tight. I usually stick my half Chizler in there and loosen it up. By doing this you are making it easier on yourself to install the film. But remember when you are doing this that you are loosening the dirt in the gaskets as well; that is why it's one of the first things that I do. It's always best to get all of the dirt out with your Chizler from the gaskets before the final squeegee.

Next, I re-spray the window.

After spraying the quarter window, I use my retractable razor blade on the window.

Now I squeegee the quarter window with my small yellow squeegee.

How to clean the back window

Start by spraying the back window with
your solution.

Get your scrub pad and scrub the whole
window with your pad. I use the scrub pad
to clean the back windows because you don't
want to damage the defroster lines if you
use razor blades, you will damage them.

Spray the glass again with your solution
and then squeegee it from left to right
all the way across. Do it as far as you
can go.

Once you can't go any further, use your side sweeper to squeegee the rest of the window.

After I'm done squeegeing it, I grab my rag and go over the sides with it. By doing this I'm getting rid of any leftover dirt.

Spray the sides with your solution, flushing the dirt down the window. Then spray the back of the window, preparing it to install the back film.

Chapter 6

Step Four Installing the Film

In this section, I will teach you how to install the film properly. This is one of the most important basic steps you must master to achieve a pro-style installation.

Side Windows..........................66

Quarter Windows...................75

Back Windows.......................76

Installing

How to install the side windows

Before you start with the next steps, I would recommend squeegeeing your glass off with the solution mixture. If this is your first install of the day, dust settles on the glass over night and when you peel the liner off it could get on to the film, making your job dirty. After cleaning your glass, peel the dull side of the film back and start to spray your solution on the sticky side of the film.

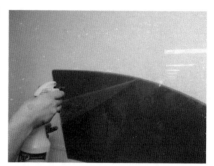

Peel it until it's two inches away from the bottom of the film. Keep spraying the solution.

Grab the film from the corner. You will have your thumb on the shiny side and your index finger on the dull side of the film. Make sure not to touch the film with your fingers. If your finger touches the film, there could be a chance that it will leave dirt on the film.

Here is a close up of me handling the film.

Once you have the corner lifted, slide your other hand underneath it. Make sure you don't touch the top with your fingers. Your fingers usually contain dirt that will make your installation dirty.

Make sure you are close to the door when you are going to install it. There is lint flying all around, so the closer you are to your window, the less lint will get between your film and the window. Have the window cleaned and ready to go.

CONTINUED ON NEXT PAGE

Install the top right corner first; slide it into the gasket.

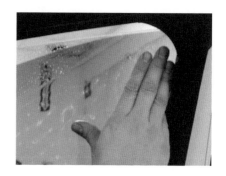

Make sure that it is snug.

After it is in the top right corner, make sure the film is in the other corner too. The middle of the film most of the time will fall in place; just make sure the two corners are where you want them to be. And you normally want the film as close as you can to the edge of the glass. The closer it is to the edge the better the installation job will look. Just don't get too close because your film could peel, I would say an eight from the edge is perfect.

Spray the film with your solution.

With your left hand's thumb, put pressure up against the film and the glass. By doing this you are holding the slippery film in place while you squeegee the film.

Keep pressure on glass and film.

Now you are ready to squeegee the film. When you are on this step, you are making sure that you are sealing the film to the glass.

CONTINUED ON NEXT PAGE

Know you want to seal the other side. Still put pressure on the film and on the glass.

After doing both top sides, you are ready to start squeegeeing down and sealing the bottom. Only go as far as the part that is not uncovered.

With your white Teflon, seal the edges of both the right and left corners.

Now you want to remove the dull side of the film completely, and with one hand, keep the film lifted while you re-spray the bottom side. I was told once to spray the bottom like I was sweeping dirt with a broom. Sweep it to the corners.

Now you are ready to install the right corner. The film will not slide in by itself, so you must learn to manipulate the film to slide it under the gasket, just make sure you don't push it all the way in just yet. This is where I use the Chizler, sometimes, or the white Teflon. It just depends on the type of gasket. I usually try both until one of them works correctly.

CONTINUED ON NEXT PAGE

Installing

After getting the right corner ready, I do the same for the other corner; just remember that I'm not pushing it all the way down the gasket just yet. I'm just getting it ready to go under the gasket.

Sometimes, I have to mess around with it until I feel that it is ready to slide in.

With both corners ready to be installed, I use my white Teflon to force the film into the gasket. By holding the white Teflon with my thumb and index finger, I use the middle finger to push the film down.

Sometimes I have to use the Chizler. I use both of these tools, but there are a lot of different tools that are designed to do the same thing. You might have to experiment and choose the one that is right for you.

Once the film is completely under the bottom gasket, you are ready to squeegee the rest of the bottom part. When you are squeegeeing, make sure to overlap so you don't leave any bubbles behind.

CONTINUED ON NEXT PAGE

Once I'm done squeegeeing the bottom part, I usually go over the gasket with my Chizler just to make sure that no fingers pop back up. If they do I will grab my heat gun and heat the little fingers from the inside. I just make sure I never hold the heat gun over the door panel for too long. If you do this, make sure you don't burn the door panel.

After I'm done installing the window tint, I usually wipe down the door panels with my microfiber cloths, customers appreciate that, then I go back and heat up the corners from the out side of the window. When I'm heating up the corners from the out side of the window, on most cars that have plastic side moldings, I use an old black Teflon that I use to shield the plastic from the heat of the heat gun. If you don't do this, you could end up melting the side molding and getting a very angry customer. I also check for lint and dirt trapped in between the film and the glass. With the heat gun and your Chizler, you should be able to heat up the dirt and lint, pressing out the air trapped in between the glass and film. You must check it really well.

How to install the quarter windows

The quarter windows are installed the same way as the side windows: peel the dull side, wet the film, and try installing it without touching anything. Apply the film directly to the glass and use your Chizler when you need to get it under the gasket, and in between the gaskets. Then you use your squeegee to squeegee out the solution.

1.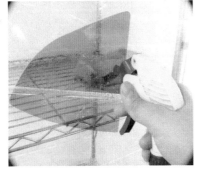

2.

3.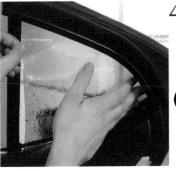

4.

5.

CONTINUED ON NEXT PAGE

Installing

How to install the back window

You should have your back window shrunk, cleaned, and ready to be installed. I usually place it on my glass face up.

While on the glass, I peel the dull side of the film off, exposing the sticky side of the film. I spray the whole film with my solution.

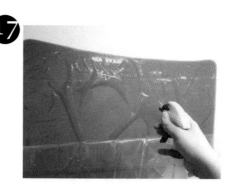

Once the film is sprayed with the solution, it is ready to be installed. I never grab the back window with my fingers. I usually use my nail to touch the film. I remove the film with my right hand and slide my left hand underneath it. If done correctly you should have the film over both your arms.

You should have the film like I do in this picture. The car should be close to the glass that you are using to install the film. The closer to the glass, the less lint you will pick up.

Slide into the backseat, making sure your film doesn't touch anything in the process, and slide the film as low as you can before tacking the top part down.

CONTINUED ON NEXT PAGE

Installing

When you are installing the back window, go as low as you can and lead with the corners before laying the top part down. The film is just much easier to handle when you do this.

Once the bottom is under the matrix, look at the top and make sure no light is coming through it. Make sure it covers an eight over the top that should keep it from having light coming through.

Once the film is in place, I like to squeegee the middle to tack the film in place.

Once I have the middle tacked down, I like to squeegee from side to side. I start from the top and go as low as I can.

When I can't get any lower, I use my side sweeper to finish the bottom.

If any fingers pop up at the bottom, I use my slim foot. Sometimes I put a rag on the tip and use that to soak up extra solution from the bottom of the back window.

CONTINUED ON NEXT PAGE

Installing

After I'm finished squeegeeing down the whole back window, I usually get a piece of black Teflon covered in a rag and go over all of the sides. I do this to make sure that it won't come back up on the sides.

Once I tack down the sides, I clean the back window once more so that I can check it. I look for fingers, dirt and lint that might be trapped underneath it.

1.   2.   3.

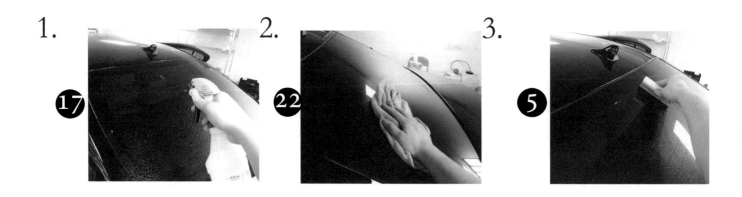

If I have any fingers that pop back up, I burn them out from the outside of the window. Then I go back in with my black Teflon rapped in a rag and push it out. The heat usually warms the glue, making it stick better. When you first start doing this, it is always good to count how long you've been holding the heat on the outside. I usually hold it for about five to six seconds, but count and adjust as needed.

You can also use this trick to burn out lint and dirt. You can never remove the dirt completely, but you can burn the extra air trapped along the dirt to make it less noticeable. The same goes with the lint, just remember to count. If you hold it for too long, you can burn the film. I did this once or twice, and that's why I count. If it gets too hot, spray the window with your solution.

Conclusion

If you have correctly followed the steps I have demonstrated, you should have a finished product similar to the one I have down below. I created this book to help guide you through the process of window tinting your own car and getting comfortable using all the tools I used in each step. The four basic steps to window tinting are what every beginner must know. I would recommend practicing because the more you practice the better you will get. My hope is that I have provided you with all the information you need to succeed, so that you can enjoy all the benefits of window tinting; furthermore, I would also like to wish you good luck on your journey through the process of learning to window tint.

32654477R00049

Made in the USA
Lexington, KY
28 May 2014